KNOW

Turning *the* Christian Life

BE

Right Side Up

DO

LARRY ALAN THOMPSON

eternity
resources

Eternity Resources books may be ordered through booksellers or by contacting:

resources

A division of Eternity Communications, Inc.
467 W 2nd Street
Lexington, KY 40507
www.eternityresources.com
(859) 327-3337

ISBN: 978-0-692-70599-5

STUDY OUTLINE

WELCOME TO THE KNOW BE DO BIBLE STUDY

It's really not about studying the *Bible*. It's not even about *studying* God.

It's about *knowing* Him.

The more you *know* God, the more you'll know yourself—*being* who you truly are in Christ and *doing* what only He can do through you.

Know. Be. Do.

It's revolutionarily simple. And simply revolutionary. So get ready for an ever-fascinating journey of walking the Christian life right side up. And remember, the journey *is* the destination. So take your time, cherish every moment spent getting to know the Creator, and prepare to enjoy a guided tour with God that will help you discover a whole new perspective on your Christian walk.

PURPOSE

The *Know Be Do Bible Study Resource* is a tool to help you get the most from your experience of reading *Know Be Do: Turning the Christian Life Right Side Up*. Whether you go through it individually or as part of a group, these sessions will help you dive deeper into the Know Be Do concepts and apply them to your life.

LEADER SUGGESTIONS

Going through *Know Be Do* as a group—whether a small group or an entire church—is the best way to experience the transformation the study offers. As a leader, you can help encourage community and life change and enhance the group experience. Here are some suggestions:

1. Make the class interactive and participatory. Participants will learn from you and each other.

2. Session 1 requires no preparation on the participant's part. This introductory session is a time for participants to get to know one another and begin bonding, and it makes a good time to distribute books and resource booklets which will be needed to prepare for Session 2. At the end of Session 1, ask participants to complete Session 2 as their "homework." Then, during Session 2, go over the homework in class, asking participants to share their answers and what they've learned and experienced. Follow this pattern throughout the following 12 weeks.

3. Use social media to enrich the group experience. Set up a Know Be Do Study Group on Facebook or other interactive website. Make it a place where participants can share insights, inspiration, and news about the class. Also, encourage participants to share comments on their own social media about how God is working in their lives. Suggest that they use **#knowbedo** in their posts so others can find them.

4. Encourage each participant use *Know Be Do* to disciple a friend, either during or after the study. Teaching truths that you've learned is one of the best ways to cement the concepts in your own life.

INTRODUCTION

READ

▶ 1 John 1

RESPOND

The Apostle John is the *know* author of the Bible. He uses the word *know* about twice as often as the average New Testament author. He truly *knew* Christ. In 1 John 1:1–4, he likens himself to a "witness." Like a witness in a court of law, John simply describes what he heard, saw, and felt. Think of yourself as a witness (*be* a witness). Make a simple list of what you have heard, seen, and felt about God (*know*).

In spiritual darkness, it's hard to hear, see, or feel God; that's why it's hard to fellowship with Him (@1 John 1:6). In the light, we can experience Him and have fellowship with Him. Describe times in your life when you've been in the light and in fellowship with God. Describe times when you've been in spiritual darkness. How have these experiences helped you to *know* God better.

Pick an attribute of God—any attribute—His grace, for example. Explain why it is particularly meaningful to you (*know*). As a believer, do you possess that attribute in some degree (*be*)? In what ways have you lived out that attribute in your daily life (*do*)?

REFLECT

As you begin this study, tell a friend about the journey on which you're about to embark. Invite them to pray for you during the study—or even to join you in it! The accountability, sharing, and fellowship will enrich your experience.

Session 2

JOURNEY AND KNOW

READ

▶ Prologue (pp. vii–viii)
▶ Chapter 1—My Journey (pp. 3–9)
▶ Chapter 2—Know (pp. 10–24)

RESPOND

Describe your own journey in the Christian walk? Has it been steady growth? Roller coaster? All uphill? Too many valleys, not enough mountaintops? What milestones have you passed?

On which do you focus most—Know, Be, or Do?

In what ways are you involved in each one?

Find a verse or passage that shows the importance of knowing God. How does it teach you to know God better?

Find a verse that shows one or more of the five ways God reveals Himself.

Read 1 John 5:13–20. Underline or make a note of each time John uses the word *know*. The first six times John uses *know*, it's the ordinary word for *know* (*eido*). The last time (v. 20—"so that we may *know* the true One.") John uses a different word for *know* (*ginosko*).Why do you think that one is different?

Look up Luke 1:34, Matthew 7:23, and John 10:27. What do these "knows" share in common with 1 John 5:20?

What do you think is man's highest calling? Give a verse to support it.

How can knowing God help you answer that calling?

REFLECT

As you listen to messages in church and read passages this week, look for Know Be Do. Write down a few ways you see Know, Be, and/or Do in sermons and Scripture this week.

If there's a particular thought or insight you learned this week, share it on your Know Be Do Study Group page, your own social media (use #knowbedo), or with a friend.

Session 3

BE AND DO

READ

▶ Chapter 3—Be (pp. 25–39)
▶ Chapter 4—Do (pp. 40–54)

RESPOND

Make a list of 10 things that make you feel valuable? Be honest with yourself. Don't say what you think *should* be true, but what is really true.

1.   6.

2.   7.

3.   8.

4.   9.

5.   10.

Read the following verses: 2 Corinthians 5:21; Colossians 3:3–4; Hebrews 10:19–22. Use these—and other verses if you like—and make a list of 10 things that define you in God's eyes.

1.   6.

2.   7.

3.   8.

4.   9.

5.   10.

Compare your two lists. Which points overlap? Which points conflict? Which points will matter 100 years from now?

Read over the four statements that start with "I..." on page 34 (from *The Search for Significance*). Write them on something (card, computer, phone) where you will see them often. Pause several times a day to read them and let them soak in.

KNOW BE DO

Satan is a liar and a master of disguise (John 8:44; 2 Corinthians 11:14). Name a half dozen or so ways that he regularly lies and deceives you.

Find a verse that tells the truth about each of these lies.

True or false test:

1. My obedience is motivated by love for God, not how it looks to man. ○ True ○ False
2. I am more interested in getting to know God than earning brownie points to win His favor. ○ True ○ False
3. When doing ministry, I proactively seek God's will for my life, not merely react to needs. ○ True ○ False
4. I spend more time cultivating a relationship with God than crafting a godly PR image on social media. ○ True ○ False
5. I feel better about myself when I consider how much God loves me than when I've done something really nice for someone. ○ True ○ False
6. I behave the same when only God is looking as when all eyes are on me. ○ True ○ False

For every "False" answer, find at least one verse that gives you—not a command—but simply a truth about God to *know*. Meditate on the verse(s) and how you can reflect that quality. Here are a couple for starters: 1 Thessalonians 2:4; Galatians 1:10.

REFLECT

As you go through your week, be on the lookout for lies that Satan tries to feed you. Jot them down along with a Scripture that corrects the error.

If there's a particular thought or insight you learned this week, share it on your Know Be Do Study Group page, your own social media (use #knowbedo), or with a friend.

Session 4

KNOW BE DO BIBLE STUDY METHOD

READ

▶ Chapter 20—Know Be Do Bible Study Method (pp. 245–260)
▶ Appendices A, B, C, and D (pp. 265–277)

RESPOND

After you finish the reading assignment, complete studies of two different passages using the Know Be Do Bible Study Method. Make notes using the charts on the following two pages (Know Be Do Bible Study Journal pages).

Your first passage is Joshua 1:1–9.

Your second passage is one of your own choosing. Select a passage that's about one or two paragraphs. One or two *verses* is usually too short. One or two *chapters* is usually too long. For this second study, consider selecting a passage from the New Testament.

A third Know Be Do Bible Study Journal page is also provided for your ongoing study. Feel free to make unlimited copies for your use. You can also download the page at **LarryAlanThompson.com/KnowBeDoJournalpage**.

REFLECT

As you listen to messages in church and read passages this week, think about them through the Know Be Do Bible Study lens. Make simple Know Be Do charts for the various passages you encounter this week.

If there's a particular thought or insight you learned this week, share it on your Know Be Do Study Group page, your own social media (use #knowbedo), or with a friend.

PASSAGE   Joshua 1:1–9

▲ KNOW   ■ BE   ● DO

CONNECTING THE DOTS

PASSAGE

▲ KNOW	■ BE	● DO

CONNECTING THE DOTS

PASSAGE ....

▲ KNOW	■ BE	● DO

CONNECTING THE DOTS ....

....

....

....

GOD—ILLUMINATION AND GOD'S KINDNESS

READ

▶ Chapter 5—God—Illumination (pp. 57–72)
▶ Chapter 6—God's Kindness (pp. 73–83)

RESPOND

Think about someone you know better than anyone else. List three things you know about them that no one else knows.

Name an attribute about God that has impressed you lately. Explain why. Find a verse that speaks about that quality.

Read Romans 8:11. Does God's Spirit live in you? If so, name at least one way in which you are different now than "B.C." (Before Christ). Focus on *being*, not doing.

Think about the last time you really failed as a Christian. Read John 15:5. How could applying that truth have changed the outcome? Again, think more in terms of *knowing* God and *being* who you are in Him, than what you could have *done* differently.

List three or more examples of God's kindness that you seldom consider. Spend a moment thanking and praising God for them. Find a verse that speaks of one or more of these qualities.

Think about someone who has wronged or offended you, perhaps someone with whom you are still bitter. What is their offense? Read Ephesians 4:32. Think of the worst way that you believe you have sinned against God. Which of these two offenses is greater? Which is forgiven?

Read Matthew 5:16. Name three ways that you reflect a distorted image of God to others. Name three ways you reflect a glorifying image of God to others. Name three more ways that you could reflect more compassion, forgiveness, grace, and kindness. Again, think *be*, then *do*.

REFLECT

Begin a running list this week of as many examples of God's kindness as you can. Remember the example of the professor and the fish from pages 61–62. Don't stop at a short list. Keep looking, looking, looking...

If there's a particular thought or insight you learned this week, share it on your Know Be Do Study Group page, your own social media (use #knowbedo), or with a friend.

GOD'S POWER AND INTELLIGENCE

READ

▶ Chapter 7—God's Power (pp. 84–95)
▶ Chapter 8—God's Intelligence (pp. 96–107)

RESPOND

Think about a time when you were at the end of your rope. You had nowhere and no one to turn to. How did (or how could have) God's power redeem the situation?

Read Ephesians 1:18–22. Use the Know Be Do Bible Study Method to unpack this brief passage.

Read the story about "Mr. Pike" on page 93. Then make a list of at least three ways that your life resembles Mr. Pike's, that is, thought patterns that are in a rut which could be transformed by God's truths. Then find a verse(s) that helps you reprogram your *being*.

Read 1 Corinthians 1:26–31. Contrast the two views of yourself:

World's view of you	God's view of you

We live in an upside-down world which Jesus came to make right side up. Describe some things in this world that are upside-down.

Read James 3:17. Make a list of wisdom's attributes and post them in a place where you will see them often during the week. Focus on letting these qualities transform your outlook each day.

REFLECT

During the week, be aware of areas where your worldview is upside down in comparison to God's view. Keep a running list. Focus on one or two and find a verse(s) that portrays God's right-side-up viewpoint. Then ask Him to help you *be* it and *do* it.

If there's a particular thought or insight you learned this week, share it on your Know Be Do Study Group page, your own social media (use #knowbedo), or with a friend.

GOD'S CONNECTIVITY AND ETERNALITY

READ

▶ Chapter 9—God's Connectivity (pp. 108–122)
▶ Chapter 10—God's Eternality (pp. 123–133)

RESPOND

Imagine what the world would look like if God had never revealed Himself. Describe what you think the world would be like. What would your life be like?

Read John 1:1–23. Make a list of every word that communicates God revealing Himself to man. (For example, Word, light, witness, etc.)

God created us to be in community, in one accord. Read through the list of "one anothers" on pages 120–121. Write down the three that you best exemplify. Write down the three that you least exemplify. Fostering a sense of community, how could you improve in the three areas in which you need help? Be specific.

God cares more about His glory than our timetable. Time is just a tool to Him. Think of a time when He seemed to show up late. Did He ultimately get glory from the situation? What is He "late" to now? How might He get glory from the waiting?

Read Matthew 6:19–21, 24. What are the risks of an investment in Earthly Treasures? What are the risks of an investment in Heavenly Treasures? Where are you making the most investments (*do*)? According to verses 21 and 24, where is your heart (*be*)? What do you *know* about God that makes an investment in Heavenly Treasures less risky and more rewarding?

Take a vision test. Close your eyes and think about at least three things that will be of the most value to you 100 years from now. Then open your eyes and think about three things that seem valuable now, but will be worthless in 100 years. How could a deeper relationship with God help correct your vision?

REFLECT

During the week, ask God to show you someone with whom He wants you to connect. It may be a believer or nonbeliever, someone in your church or outside it. Reach out to that person this week and set up a time, perhaps lunch or other activity, when you can get to know one another.

If there's a particular thought or insight you learned this week, share it on your Know Be Do Study Group page, your own social media (use #knowbedo), or with a friend.

Session 8

GOD'S SERVICE AND PURITY

READ

▶ Chapter 11—God's Service (pp. 134–145)
▶ Chapter 12—God's Purity (pp. 146–159)
▶ Conclusion of Book Two (pp. 160–163)

RESPOND

Read Philippians 2:3–8. Then hook yourself up to the "spiritual heart cath" (see pp. 136–137). What evidences of Christian consumerism do you see in your life with regard to your church? With regard to God?

Pages 139–144 describe three types of people:

1. **You serve me.**—"What's yours is mine."

2. **You serve me, and I'll serve you.**—"What's yours is yours. What's mine is mine."

3. **I'll serve you.**—"What's mine is yours."

Read Luke 10:25–37. Which type of person were the robbers? Which type were the priest and Levite? Which type was the Samaritan? Which type are you? Why?

Think of someone in Scripture who was a true servant. How could you *know* God better as they knew God/Christ? How could you reflect God's character to *be* more servant hearted? How could you follow their example to *do* acts of service?

KNOW BE DO

True or false test:

1. *My* sin—not someone else's sin—typically makes me angry at sin.   ○ True ○ False
2. I rarely try to justify my sin.   ○ True ○ False
3. I consistently view my sin as self-destructive.   ○ True ○ False
4. I frequently think about God's holiness in contrast to my sin.   ○ True ○ False
5. I often consider the truth that God lives within me before I sin.   ○ True ○ False
6. I regularly take sinful thoughts captive before succumbing to sin.   ○ True ○ False

If you had any "False" answers, find a verse from God's Word that helps you *know* how God views sin. If you had only "True" answers, read Proverbs 16:18.

Read 2 Corinthians 5:21. How do you become (*be*) the righteousness of God...Your performance? Or your position in Christ? How does that truth impact what you *do* on a daily basis?

Read through Psalm 51. *Who* does the washing, cleansing, purging, blotting out, cleaning, and restoring...you or God? What is the final result of the cleansing according to verses 12–15?

REFLECT

As you go through your week, practice the discipline of taking spiritual "showers" quickly after you sin. Immediately get clean with God by claiming the promises of Scriptures such as Psalm 51 and 1 John 1:9. How does *being* and feeling consistently clean affect what you *do* during the week?

If there's a particular thought or insight you learned this week, share it on your Know Be Do Study Group page, your own social media (use #knowbedo), or with a friend.

US—INSPIRATION AND KNOWING GOD'S WILL

READ

▶ Chapter 14—Us—Inspiration (pp. 167–168)
▶ Chapter 15—Knowing God's Will (pp. 169–185)

RESPOND

Write down three "What ifs" for your life. Not regrets looking back at the past, but exciting possibilities for the future—God-sized potential stories for the rest of your life. Keep these "What ifs" in mind as you work through the rest of this lesson.

If God's will is found in a Person (Christ), not a place or thing, in what ways should that affect the way you go about knowing God's will?

The book lists five ways to miss God's will. Think of a situation in your past when you made a bad decision because of one of these five ways:

1. Too focused on the future

2. Not asking for guidance

3. Emotional decision

4. Circumstantial evidence

5. Acting too fast—or too slow

How could have a focus on *knowing* God and *being* who you are in Christ have made a difference in one or more of these situations. Use Scripture, such as Proverbs 3:5–6, to solidify your point.

Discerning God's will involves lining up three "lights." Think about a decision you're facing right now. Consider input from these three sources and jot down a note about each point. What direction or course of action is lining up with all three?

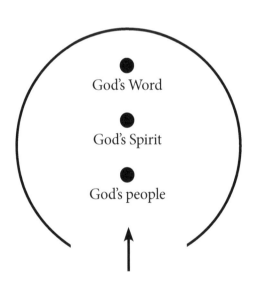

REFLECT

As you go through your week, pause each day and think about decisions you made during the day. Ask yourself two questions about each one:

1. Did I make a wrong decision due to one of the five errors above?

2. How would knowing God better (through His Word, His Spirit, and His people) have made a difference in the decision?

If there's a particular thought or insight you learned this week, share it on your Know Be Do Study Group page, your own social media (use #knowbedo), or with a friend.

OVERCOMING STUBBORN SIN

READ

▶ Chapter 16—Overcoming Stubborn Sin (pp. 186–200)

RESPOND

Read Psalm 32:1–5. Think about the stubborn sins in your life, the ones you tend to commit over and over. List the top three stubborn sins in your life.

1.

2.

3.

Focus on the #1 stubborn sin in your life, the one the Bible calls a besetting sin (Hebrews 12:1). Create a chart like the one on page 192. On the left side, list everything you know about God and His truth as it relates to your sin. On the right side, list Satan's lies that conflict with each truth. List at least five truth–lie pairs. Apply the Know Be Do concept to turn your thinking about this sin right side up.

God Knowledge	Satan's Lies
1.	
2.	
3.	
4.	
5.	

Focus on God's Perspective. Read Romans 8:15–16. How does a focus on His fatherly attitude towards us (His love, wrath, grief, grace, mercy, forgiveness) change your attitude toward your sin?

Focus on God's Presence. Read John 14:15–21. How does a focus on His intimate presence in you and you in Him (His purity, power, perseverance) change your attitude toward your sin?

Focus on God's Promises. Read Matthew 11:28–29. What are the two imperatives in these verses? (Refer to pp. 198–200.)

What are the two indicatives (promises)?

How does a focus on His promises change your attitude toward your sin?

REFLECT

Think about your besetting sin. Find a verse(s) in the Bible with an imperative-indicative that offers you God's perspective, presence, and promises, helping His truth win out over Satan's lies with regard to your sin. Example: 1 Peter 5:7.

If there's a particular thought or insight you learned this week, share it on your Know Be Do Study Group page, your own social media (use #knowbedo), or with a friend.

ANSWERING LIFE'S DOUBTS WITH FAITH

READ

▶ Chapter 17—Answering Life's Doubts with Faith (pp. 201–213)

RESPOND

Have you ever had a "crisis of faith"? What was the outcome? Do you have any lingering doubts? What are they?

Read Hebrews 11:1 and 2 Corinthians 4:18 and 5:7. In your own words, write a definition of faith that encompasses what these and other Scriptures describe.

How does faith enable you to experience (*ginosko*) God through your spirit (*know*)?

How does faith enable you to experience (*ginosko*) God through your being (*be*)?

How does faith enable you to experience (*ginosko*) God through your doing (*do*)?

The chapter describes three types of questions: distorted questions, discovery questions, and difficult questions. Think about your own doubts concerning God, perhaps "unanswered" prayers, "unexplainable" questions about the Bible, "unresolved" disappointments in life. As you think about these doubts...

...in what ways are your doubts a result of Satan's distorted questions, such as, "Did God really say...?" List Satan's distorted questions to you.

...in what ways are your doubts addressed by God's discovery questions, such as "Where are you?..." List God's discovery questions to you.

...in what ways are your doubts sincere expressions of difficult questions you may have, such as "Where is God when...?" Pray and ask God to show you answers. Write down Scriptures and insights that He brings to mind.

REFLECT

As you go through your week, be sensitive to others around you and their doubts and unbelief about God. Ask the Lord to help you give an answer to those doubts and express your own faith in God, perhaps sharing a reassuring Scripture. Make some notes of your experiences.

If there's a particular thought or insight you learned this week, share it on your Know Be Do Study Group page, your own social media (use #knowbedo), or with a friend.

Session 12

KNOW BE DO AND YOUR SPIRITUAL AND EARTHLY LIFE

READ

▶ Chapter 18—Know Be Do and Your Spiritual Life (pp. 214–229)
▶ Chapter 19—Know Be Do and Your Earthly Life (pp. 230–244)

RESPOND

We are often bombarded with "flash bangs" (see pp. 214–215) that are tossed into our lives by the world, leaving us stunned, numb, off-balance, blind and deaf to God. What are some of the flash bangs in your life that distract you from *ginosko* knowing God?

Below are the 10 facets of your life mentioned in these two chapters. For each one, give yourself a grade (A, B, C, D, E) on how well you are focused on knowing God in that area vs. merely doing the activity, i.e., how well your identity is aligned with your ideal (p. 232). Then, write down one simple, specific way you can improve and search for a verse that will inspire you toward that end.

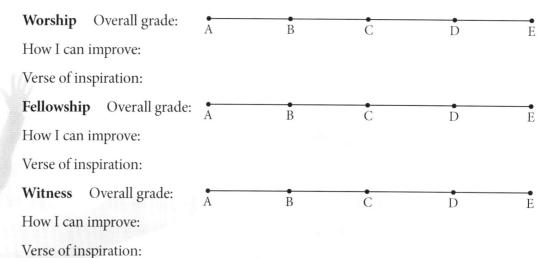

Worship   Overall grade: A — B — C — D — E

How I can improve:

Verse of inspiration:

Fellowship   Overall grade: A — B — C — D — E

How I can improve:

Verse of inspiration:

Witness   Overall grade: A — B — C — D — E

How I can improve:

Verse of inspiration:

KNOW BE DO

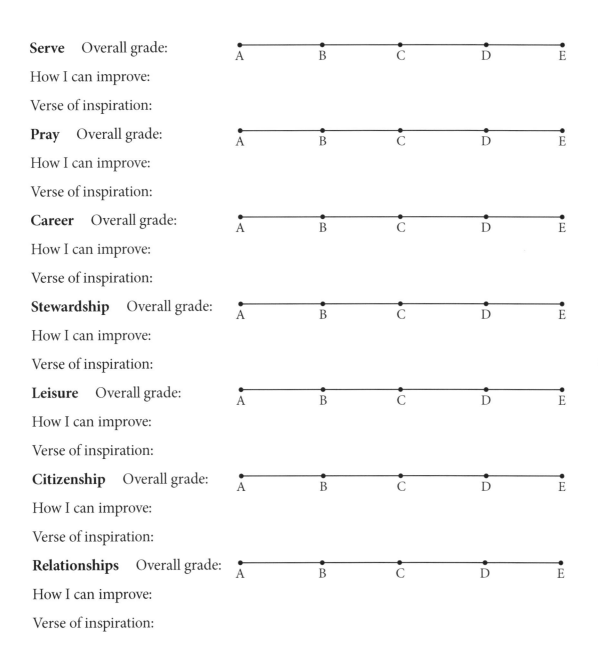

Serve   Overall grade:

How I can improve:

Verse of inspiration:

Pray   Overall grade:

How I can improve:

Verse of inspiration:

Career   Overall grade:

How I can improve:

Verse of inspiration:

Stewardship   Overall grade:

How I can improve:

Verse of inspiration:

Leisure   Overall grade:

How I can improve:

Verse of inspiration:

Citizenship   Overall grade:

How I can improve:

Verse of inspiration:

Relationships   Overall grade:

How I can improve:

Verse of inspiration:

REFLECT

Next time you spend time in worship—either in corporate worship at church or personal worship—take a few periodic readings on your "true worship meter" (see p. 219). Don't be so self-aware and introspective that you lose focus on worship. But use it to discover how much true *ginosko* knowing God you are experiencing during worship. Record your observations.

If there's a particular thought or insight you learned this week, share it on your Know Be Do Study Group page, your own social media (use #knowbedo), or with a friend.

KNOW BE DO BIBLE STUDIES

READ

▶ Epilogue (pp. 261–263)
▶ Reread, if desired, Chapter 20—Know Be Do Bible Study Method (pp. 245–260)
▶ Reread, if desired, Appendices A, B, C, and D (pp. 265–277)

RESPOND

As your "final exam" for this study, think of a topic in your life about which you would like God to teach you more. The topic might be one His attributes, such as His kindness, power, purity, or other quality. The topic might be a question or decision you're facing. The topic might be a sin with which you are struggling. Once you've settled on your topic, identify a Scripture passage that addresses your topic. Use a Bible concordance, online search tools, or ask a mature believer to point you to an appropriate passage. Finally, conduct a full Know Be Do Bible Study using the method we learned in Chapter 20 and the appendices. Make this study a model for other Bible studies you'll do as you continue your spiritual journey with God.

REFLECT

As you listen to messages in church and read passages this week, think about them through the Know Be Do Bible Study lens. Make simple Know Be Do charts for the various passages you encounter this week.

Use this final session to reflect on what you've learned about God and yourself. Share these thoughts with someone. How has the study impacted your life? What goals will you set for continuing to use the Know Be Do concept in your spiritual walk?

PASSAGE

▲ KNOW	■ BE	● DO

CONNECTING THE DOTS

K N O W

Acknowledge His attributes | Awareness of His presence

B E

Abide in His ability | Acceptance of your position in Him

D O

Act on His authority | Appropriation of His power

Made in the USA
Columbia, SC
11 August 2024